CW00766755

New and Selected Poems

MOLLY HOLDEN

SELECTED POEMS

CARCANET

First published in 1987 by
CARCANET PRESS LIMITED
208-212 Corn Exchange, Manchester M4 3BQ
and 198 Sixth Avenue, New York, NY 10013

Copyright © Alan Holden 1987

All rights reserved.

British Library Cataloguing in Publication Data

Holden, Molly
 Selected poems.
 I. Title
 821'.914   PR6058.043

 ISBN 0-85635-696-4

The publisher acknowledges the financial assistance of the
Arts Council of Great Britain.

Typeset in 10pt Palatino by Bryan Williamson, Manchester
Printed in England by SRP Ltd, Exeter

A Note

The poems selected here form about a sixth of Molly Holden's work. They are taken from pamphlets, books, journals and manuscript sources; firstly, an early printed pamphlet, *A Hill Like a Horse* (1963) and an Outposts booklet, *The Bright Cloud* (1964); secondly, the three collections published by Chatto and Windus: *To Make Me Grieve* (1968), *Air and Chill Earth* (1971), and *The Country Over* (1975); thirdly, "uncollected" poems published in journals around 1976-8; and finally (about 400 in all) unpublished poems extant in typescript or single manuscript sheets or in eight note-books. This adds up to over 600 poems, which were put into order by Alan Holden after her death from multiple sclerosis in 1981.

Her first two Chatto collections received some notice and sold well; the acceptance of the "uncollected" poems was an index of growing esteem for her work. Since that time, when she was less and less able to write and send poems out, her work faded from public view. It is our purpose to bring her poetry, in a "selected" edition, back to the notice of readers.

SIMON CURTIS

Contents

Worcestershire Lanes

This country differs from dry uplands, water hereabouts
is no white rarity. The muddy ditch
the Saxons named still moves beside the road
and milking-time soon churns the yard to sludge.

Men could build where they would; farms
five fields apart and cottages in threes up tracks
now detail slope and hollow, and lanes mizmaze
the countryside, hedges a screen for lover and for fox.

Thorn, hazel, briar make them alike, easy
to lose one's way, different in small things only –
empty beehives in a gangling orchard, a church
with no apparent parish, shock-yewed and lonely.

Sometimes these lanes go by, irrelevant as thoughts,
for miles with only magpies, padlocked gate, and crop,
a philosophic pattern to the man born locally,
to others only metaphors without a map.

Barn Roof

A roof bedevils me, sagging
condemned above arcaded barn, worked on
by time and weather to more than
artifact, to presence of natural beauty.
Lichened celadon and cinnabar, it
forms with clouds continuous patterns,
its mosses, runnels of rain-stains sustaining
the decorative features, the droppings of birds
more white and permanent along that ridge
than ever on branches. All
the ten tints that smear its shining tiles
in the low sunlight after rain nag me
to preserve appearances. This is
my succubus, my incandescent stack
at sunset, my shifting pool of lilies,
and my words quite without either
Monet's power of paint or perseverance
to attempt immortalising the
quarried colours, the partiality of light
for summits and decay.

Messengers

A charm of goldfinches descended
on the garden. They had the curious air
of being outriders for some royal progress,
calling across to each other sharply,
investigating hawthorns and laurel thicket,
swinging to peer on the apple trees, busy
as officials that must make no mistake.

Their black and gold was Tudor tawdry,
they swaggered. As it happened, nothing followed;
anything, after these, would have been small beer.

Country Journeys

Guide book in mind, I quiz
the charming villages, admiring,
as I must, the balance, texture, shape,
cruck, quoin, and pargetting,

but cannot see them only with
an architect's or aesthete's eye, am
already involved. That shadowed gate's
familiar underneath my hand,

hollyhocks there will need a stake,
that path's crumbling has wanted care
for years. I might have lived there
half a century, I recognise each glimpse,

can feel the draught on the
black-stockinged ankles, know the scent
of lilac phantasmal against the hedge,
have cut the briars back that will grow again.

I arrive at the end of journeys
prostrate with experience, my backside
stiff, my humanity overflowing,
my self plural with participation.

Chrysanthemums

Chrysanthemums – like courtiers
in a dying kingdom, still fantastic
in bronze or golden ruff, with hanging sleeves
of ragged green, still aping
fertility's magnificence –

bold and brilliant in the last warmth
of the sun's shorter journeys, are
either spurred to this last acrid excess
of beauty by decay's imminent arrival
or are quite unaware of the frost's fingers,
still light, still tentative, but soon
to grip the roots, to turn the leaves
sage-side up, to wither the last bright blossom.

Photograph of Haymaker, 1890

It is not so much the image of the man
that's moving – he pausing from his work
to whet his scythe, trousers tied
below the knee, white shirt lit by
another summer's sun, another century's –
as the sight of the grasses beyond
his last laid swathe, so living yet
upon the moment previous to death;
for as the man stooping straightened up
and bent again they died before his blade.

Sweet hay and gone some seventy years ago
and yet they stand before me in the sun,
stems damp still where their neighbours' fall
uncovered them, succulent and straight,
immediate with moon-daisies.

Hare

He lives on edge throughout his days,
home-fixated, short of sight,
dark heart beating as to burst his breast,
given to sudden panic fright
that sends him hurtling unpredictably
through crops, round quarries, over stones.
And has great eyes, all veined with blood,
and beautifully-articulated bones.

Superstition gives him an unchancy name,
any power that you might mention;
certainly he haunts the corner of the eye,
the edge of the attention
on open downs where movement is surprising,
caught and gone again with every glance,
or jack-knifing quietly through adjacent hedges
beyond the golden stubble-fires' dance.

But he is no more than flesh and blood,
living all his speedy life with fear,
only oblivious of constant danger
at his balletic time of year
when spring skies, winds, the greening furrows
overcome hunger, nervousness, poor sight,
fill him with urgent, huge heroics,
make him stand up and fight.

Ad Limitem

A sprinkle of salt, the core of an apple
might have placated whatever lived
in that damp and barren bit
between the last council house and the first
fields. Boundary country it was,
where men built altars once to sacrifice
to the gods of the edges of things – of the limits
of ploughed land, the stream
from the wooded hill, the borders of marshes.
Anything would have done.

                  For a convalescing child
crouched there, alone one still grey afternoon,
by the brook of sorts that oozed below
the roots of naked thorns and splintered willow-trunks,
intent on rusty tin and hoped-for tiddlers,
and suddenly felt his bent spine prick as if
somebody watched him. He looked up,
indignant with innocence – but there was
nothing there, not even a bird
that might have startled him, nor a last leaf.

He seemed to see a shadow without
a substance in the thorns, hear an
indefinable stir along the hedge. Panic
seized him that he knew he must control.
Slowly he backed, eyes shifting along
the stream, sobs rising in his throat. He felt
behind him with his hands, touched wire, knew
this was the first fence, whirled, stumbled
for the passageway between potato plots, into
his own road, ran for his own back door and burst,
frantic, into the warm sanctuary of the tea-time fug.

Ominous with Haloes

Ominous with haloes, black
with unshed hail, the clouds race up,
obscure the sun, sweep on above the trees
whose buds glint sudden sticky gold in
sudden light again. Rooks fight
and use the gale, rearrange
their gleaming wings like tablecloths;
magpies climb white air as fish
climb streams, in pied fritillary flight,
plane down, and tumble into beeches.

Air is the dominant element today.
It moves, fills spaces furiously, is
the pure conductor of light. Scientifically,
this is what all the glitter
and speed of the morning's about.
This is the whelming breath that fills
depressions, lungs, the sails of ships,
balances desperate wings of birds;
this is the arrows on the map.
And this is the month that forces it most
on our unphilosophical attention.

Pieces of Unprofitable Land

The pieces of unprofitable land
are what I like, best seen in winter,
triangular tail of cottage garden
tall with dead willowherb, and tangled splinter
of uncut copse edging the red-ploughed fields,
and between hedge and headland of such fields
the slope of one-in-four the plough can't touch,
mayweed and old larks' nests its only yields.

In countryside so arable and fenced
that verges are the only common land
these roughs are memories of former wilds
untouched by foot, unharvested by hand.
Attained by sight alone, because so small,
private, or thorny, stuffed with the years' seeds,
their failure's proof of reclamation,
their vigour justifies all wastes and weeds.

Giant Decorative Dahlia

It is easy enough to love flowers but these
had never appealed to me before, so
out of proportion above my garden's
other coloured heads and steady stems.

This spring though, in warm soil, I set
an unnamed tuber, offered cheap, and,
when August came and still no sign,
assumed the slugs had eaten it.

                    Suddenly it showed;
began to grow, became a small tree.
It was a race between the dingy bud
and the elements. It has beaten
the frost, rears now three feet above
the muddled autumn bed, barbaric petals
pink quilled with tangerine, turning
its great innocent face towards me
triumphantly through the damp afternoon.

I could not deny it love if I tried.

Some Men Create

Some men create an unintended
   beauty by default,
never cut back the creeping ivy
   so its straggles vault

from crumbling wall to neighbouring bridge
   beside the arched lane,
to swing like hair from the parapet,
   shining with spring rain;

never gravel out the timber pile
   nor lop the dead oak
so that the seeding traveller's joy
   smothers them like smoke.

So among orderly husbandry
   leave some plots alone
that the eye may reap with pleasure what
   the hand has not sown.

New-Born

Skin sodden, genitals grotesque, the wail
of a demon, a withered face of fury
above a tiny knotted chest at odds with the world:
how love such a little animal?

but its indignation, its burning sense
of injustice! where is warmth, dark,
pulses of sustenance? why have they gone?
It is pity that possesses one at first.

And then, peaceful for the moment at the breast,
see the promise of beauty, the downy skull
– a furnace to the cheek – the arctic blue
of eyeballs. It will become human yet.

Birthplace

Two small windows, south and north, light
this shallow cottage's central room
upstairs; afternoon's sunlight streaming in
at one from orchards, fields, cottages,
all comfortable things, leaves in the other,
looking through shadow, a cool green view
of distance, the lonely heath, absorbing woods.

In this room, most probably at night,
the midwife turned, the oil-lamp flickering,
from the tired woman on the bed to
the child laid aside for dead and saw
the even fainter flicker yet of life.
Her rough hands found the breath
and helped him fight for it and so
must share to some extent, in this
small room with its mysterious two-way look
at life, the credit for our haunting
by Tess among the winter fields,
by Gabriel Oak watching Orion rise.

Every May

Every May surprises me,
   so green and white,
such bright and statelier skies
   of longer light;

cooler than I remember,
   the sun yet young,
its lily-scent amazes me,
   its dews still wrung

from dawns of misty sunlight
   when birds sing loud
and blossomed trees in orchards
   shoulder and crowd.

But now and then I notice,
   in May's sweet cold,
the comfortable heat of humans.
   I grow old.

I Grow These White Lilies

I grow these white lilies for homesickness.

Here they are set on clay, in a scoop
of midland valley, backed by a creosote fence,
luxuriant gardens. Over them droop
roses and raspberries, willow and almond tree.
This seems their element. Here they should thrive.

I grow them for this memory though – of lilies
spare as sticks, their flowers more waxenly alive
than these, by cinder paths in flat, infertile
gardens in the downs, rooted in chalk and flint,
heady and sweet by day against bare slopes,
scent and sentinel both by moonlight's glint.

These are not they, are no compensation
for those lost lilies growing in that lost land.
But, as I reach, to touch inferior petals,
I think I see the chalk beneath my hand.

The Seven Bushes

It is their colour makes them
presences, the seven standing about the bare
dark garden as gold as funeral masks.

I feel them behind my back,
uncomfortably, whenever I turn away
as if it is only the human gaze

that keeps them rooted at all.
It was always their garden as much as mine;
I have the power to kill but they to grow.

And in rain, like this, the fences
darkened, the blossom more golden than ever,
their identities are as weighty as

doubloons. They press forward.
They in their irregular stations, I in mine,
we share this soil with mutual wariness.

Ancestor

Who haunts this garden? Anne,
the wife of Robert, who never in her life
had time to spare to stand
under the apple trees or courtyard arch.
Betrothed and wed, barely out of childhood,
she bore six children, dying with the last –
her alabaster effigy, waxen
among the shadows of the church,
cradles her killer obliquely in her arms.

New hedges set a hundred years ago
do not confuse her, nor new flowers.
She takes all changes in her stride that is
thinner than wind, with neither
warmth nor weight in its pressure.
Seasons come and go, time gathers
all but a chill ghost to its end
who now has time enough but could
have used it better in a warmer life.

Discharged Seaman, 1807

Saw his child cry but did not hear
her wailing; saw sunset, heard no birds.
The cottage walled so thick, he sometimes told himself,
no sound could enter – but the door
stood open. Remembered his wife's whisper,
now only knew by movement when she spoke
or felt her fluttering throat beneath his kiss.

No blow did this – only the awful buffet
of the guns of *Victory* speaking and recoiling.
He reeled against red walls. Friends thought
him wounded, shouted, got no answer.
Through open gunports he saw battle
flaming soundlessly. Deaf as the heart
of oak itself now until the day of his death.

House Martins

All summer the house has been cocooned by
sharp sweet cries, by the invisible trajectories of wings
sweeping up to the gables, round corners, overhead.
They have also clung and sworn round each high window.

Their spittle-plastered nests are but the posting places
in lives of travelling – black far darts on shining evenings,
white bellied and rumped close to in swerving flight.
They intrude for a while and are gone without thanks.

It is said that they bring good luck in return for
hospitality but this is our seventh summer of misfortune;
it is a denial of every augury that we should be so
disturbed, bespattered, malisoned by these wild visitors.

And yet we welcome them each year, are pleased to think
our eaves and our midge-haunted garden are their
point of reference as they beat upwind along the frozen passes
of the Alps, a fledgeling memory, a shadowy ground-control.

So Which Is the Truth?

Green and differences of green
and distances and depths of green
crowd the cool gardens, the leaves lax
in their avenues, the sun in a grey cloud;
all presences are motionless, unlit.

The cloud moves on, calls up
a sudden wind that pours itself over
the hedge with just-as-sudden
sunlight, reverses the leaves, stirs shadows,
fills the blown sky with a shrill
precipitate of martins. The tipped
kaleidoscope of colour balances.

A different garden.

So which is the truth?
which is the real garden?
the confusion of sunlight
or the grey moment's attitudes?

Housesteads

This was the place I had intended
to visit all my life. Perhaps a mile
across the valley lay its stones.
I had not known it would be so far.
"You shouldn't try to do it," they all said.

But, having come to it at last, I
intended also to try; and the going
was not too bad at first, the stick
helping me. But before I began to climb
the far slope, I knew they were right.
The walls and the stone compounds
lay still ahead, the grass long, wet,
I still pretending, still making remarks.
Fool. Very little virtue in such pretences,
how much more wise to accept the
inevitable – but the stubbornness understandable?

And on the green damp slope with
such a heavy sky pressing above me, I saw
neither barrack nor guard-room, granary,
road, nor stone, only wished to be back
the other side of the valley, rested, just
looking. I forced myself on for a while
then surrendered, said
I would start making my own way back,
I would rather, they were to stay.
And I started. Forced marches must have been
just like this but I knew
I would not recover, that this was the end
of exploring, no more explanations
to children of outworks, of views, this
was what it had come to, a blind
cussedness of will, to get back, without help.
Ten steps at a time then a stop, outstaring
people coming the other way, watching
the turf, small flowers, to encourage myself,
not looking up, eyes on the few
yards ahead, no further. Then a climb,
oh god, a rising path, and this

to be tackled without pretence and my brain
black, extremity, it seemed, upon me.
Nothing walked with me, nothing sustained
despair. I do not remember
the last hundred yards save that a car
hooted so I probably wandered into the road.
And reached my beginning and so my end.

Hospital

They sought me out, the ancient consolations,
  now that I lay helpless in their reach,
with well-greased shoes and oily conversation,
  hoping to net me on that painful beach;

helpless indeed I lay, in that white bed, hands outspread,
  legs useless down the length before my eyes,
and could not care a deal for anything they said,
  kind though they thought themselves and wise.

Jamaican nurses spoke of Christ, wheelchair conversions,
  souls brought to God who'd never seen the light;
quietly I nodded when I could, without aspersions,
  was grateful that they cared to help me fight.

Catholic nurses said they'd pray for me, raising
  their rosaries, promising *aves* every day;
a priest put up a meaningless blessing, praising
  a courage I did not have, and went away.

The Church of England would have liked discussion,
  seeing I'd admitted myself: "religion none".
I held my own a while but without passion
  and asked to be excused a dialectic run.

And all the while I lay, under the words and attempted curing,
  seeking inside not out for a human grace
that would give me a strength and a courage for enduring
  against great odds in a narrow place.

The Globe

In a distant corner of some weird-landscaped
scene by Bosch there might appear
a figure in a silky bubble closed, of water,
glass, or gas, hard to identify but clear
so that his long-limbed form is seen and
probably admitting warmth and sound
as well as sight while cutting off
the prisoner from touch of hand or ground.

He braces his back and feet against the sides,
opens his mouth perhaps in grotesque crying;
there is some hope that it may burst and he
emerge, we do not know. No harm in trying.
But the globe's shatterproof in which I am
encased, all possible escape denied;
I hear and see though do not feel and may
not move, invisibly and permanently tied.

A thin membrane of difference insulates me
from my kind; and even while I sit and try to talk
of gardens, children, weather, journeys, friends,
the knowledge is perpetual that I'll never walk
again. I look and listen distantly, my self
immovable within its vacuum and quite without the hope
that keeps that painted figure struggling earnestly,
sure he may yet break skin and traverse slope.

Virtue in Necessity; from the parked car

I tire, I tire.
One place is enough for me
for an afternoon – a bridge,
a rutted gateway, a thorn.
Let me stay here while
you walk, all of you,
leave me be. Let me
contemplate being till
I grow too cold to care.

There is a virtue in
this necessity. I get to know
a tree trunk at the verge
as if I'd lived a lifetime
in its shade – disposition
of branches, ribbed bark,
the small rough leaves.
I've seen the change
of shadows round a church
that are the same
from year to year at that season,
at that slant of the sun.
It does not have to be long,
my lonely waiting, just
time enough to suck up,
to be intimate with
a kerb, a bush, action
of west wind, mortar
in brick wall, moss
or clematis on an outhouse roof.
Five minutes will do.
Five minutes will show me how
the rooks use air to rise
and fall above the elms,
on and off all day,
will show me chance,
(or call it what you will)
at work, killing
the wren on the warm road.
Half an hour

will saturate me with
the light above the choked canal
where dragonflies still glitter,
will leave me sodden
with the feel of fields,
old boundaries, freckle
my soul with the inmost
tickle of twigs in the
hazel hedge. I reflect
light from the white
and narrow puddles. I
am become the atmosphere
of villages, the varying
roofs, the ambiguous eaves.
I savour pavements and
the backsides of towns.

And am jolted back
by your return
and am tired
and have had enough
of empathy
and will go home.

Adjustment

I thought my bones would last. Good bones, I'd read,
preserve the beauty of an aged head,
and so I hoped my structure might remain
shapely, whatever age I might attain.

Skulls do not change but I'd not gauged the force
of time correctly, reckoned without the coarse
deposit of disease and grief – the double chin,
the softer jowls of middle-age, the cobwebbed skin,
that now have overlaid the thirtied grace
of what was once a pleasing enough face.

What the mirror tells me must be true. Shoulder,
breast, and sight confirm I'm getting older.

Now my portrait of myself must change, truth
forgo the bright advantages of youth.
My children see me comfortable and kind –
so there's my present image right to mind.
Shape's hoped endurance must be laid aside
and any slighter beauty that was cause for pride.

Now only I shall ever see
the fine-boned crone I'd thought to be.

Experimental Twig

Experimental twig
   planted by a child
now waves before the window,
   tree-size, and wild.

While it's been so growing
   four years in the grass
my life's been withdrawing
   into small compass.

Neither in the balance
   weighing very much
– but one has gained in beauty,
   one has lost touch.

The Crowd

A spectator at my shoulder while I read
or write I cannot bear; ironically now,
because time is short, a crowd
stands there, shadow pressing on shadow,
that I cannot gesture away nor
shrug impatiently off. They have a right
and I have an obligation.

                  What they want
and what I would attempt is
preservation of delight – no interpretation,
no claims to significance. But how perpetuate
the hawthorned quadrilaterals of
certain fields, or Wiltshire sunsets
and their cobalt resolution? how record
brown hens, dry leaves thrust by the wind
into the angles of the Temple walls,
kisses, wise quarrels, long-seeded flowers?

These are the things that persecute me,
urgently gentle, jogging
my slow elbow and murmuring:
set down our odd biographies while
there is still time, while you are still able.

Illness

Poetic justice is imperfectly exemplified in me
who, as a child, as a girl, was persuaded that
I felt as earth feels, the furrows in my flesh,

buttercups curdling from my shoulder blades,
was what I saw. The rain would fall as pertinent on me
as on the lichens on the flint-embedded wall.

I had always a skin too few, identified
with sun-hot blossom on the far side of the road,
felt beneath my own warm envelope of flesh

the foreign winter that calcined the delicate
bones of the organ-grinder's shuddering monkey.
A ploughed field poniarded my chest.

So now it seems a wry desert that youthful
ecstasies, my earthly husks of joy,
should be so turned about by this disease

that feels like mist upon my fingers, like
a cold wind for ever against my body, and
air and chill earth eternally about my bones.

Memory Without Experience

Riding back to lodgings in Salisbury one summer night,
his brain clouded with the day's memories of
heat, stones, earthworks, my grandfather
was knocked from his bike by a white owl
swooping from the dusk; so he came to his senses
in the downland grass, in a twilight without lamps,
one wheel of his overturned cycle still casually
free-wheeling itself at his side. He was a man
of little humour but laughed at himself in this,
wondered at the attack, and cycled on to rooms
where fire, meal, bed and breakfast cost five bob.

I did not even hear this from himself, it was
a secondhand experience when it came to me;
curiously I had no difficulty in seeing that
particular dusk, the sudden white shadow, and the
overturned bicycle with its slow-circling wheel.
I am not sure now that it was not myself who fell
into sweet grass in green twilight,
who remembers distinctly the bruise on the left knee.

In That Particular Bush

The north-west wind in that
particular bush divides it on the left,
folds it back upon itself, then
drops, and all the leaves
flow back again and settle
as they were until the next gust
opens it once more and the cool breath
enters.

              The motion is exciting.
If one could think so chill a thing
as wind were sexual, then this is so
and legends of miraculous conceptions
on girls who fell asleep upon
Aegean beaches, neglecting to
cross their legs when Zephyr blew,
seem almost credible, in context.

The devil's too, was cold, they used to say.

The Same Bush, In Bud

Like old gold buried long beneath the earth,
coated with verdigris and cool damp mud
above a darkly sullen gleam of worth
– wink enough to the wise – so this bush in bud

glows with the smothered light of what's to come
exampled by a few voluted flowers
already out, like prints of some damp thumb
that liquefy the grime of chthonic powers.

I wait its revelation with grave glee
as the last cleaning of rich objects found
in Wessex tombs or Bronze Age sanctuary.
No casuistry needed here – the ground

has not been robbed of sacrificial goods
that men intended for their dead's delight.
This golden bush was meant to break the clods
of my rough garden and dazzle living sight.

View from Archdeacon Fisher's Library, July 1829, by John Constable

This is more than a sketch but was never
worked up for the Academy so that it glitters
with the exact amount of white light on the leaves
that's there in truth at four o'clock in the afternoon
but is not always credited by those who look
at pictures but not at trees. He's praised
for his skies and I yield to no one in my admiration
of those clouds, building along the winds; but
until I came to watch trees with such care myself
I hadn't seen how fully he'd set down
their presences, their characters. Here,
in this sunlit meadow seen from a north window,
only a grazing horse in occupation, stand quite clearly
chestnuts at the left with their solid blocks
of leaves, an English elm in dark festoons,
an ash in the middle of the field, all
movement and sparkle. They are probably
all felled now, but he's preserved them.

                    He also preserved
with his paint, at another time, trees on a slope,
standing as if arrested on a downhill walk
because they liked the place or were
no longer thirsty for the valley stream; and only he
has ever caught the spotlit theatricality
of sunset striking up behind September branches.

Reminders

The only gulls I see now are inland
in winter, flocks that sensed the gales to come
and let the autumn's west winds carry them
to fields and reservoirs whose every strand
provides more food than does the splintering coast.
I watch them glide and tilt, their angled wings
catching the sun; their winter silence hangs
above me too. O tides and sounds I've lost!

Poets had used sea-imagery and lore
long before they learned that, in pre-human time,
man had crawled out, prone and handless, from its slime.
These are familiar themes – sea-blink and roar;
so my precedent's an exiled Saxon's words
speaking of storms and splendour of white birds.

Surely Only A Fancy

A tree like a flame in the hedge.

Crack Willow. Nothing else, save pear, has bark
so deeply fissured and pear's more regular,
its cracks in latitude and longitude, lozenges,
rectangles, plateaux of outer rind rooted in pith.
But this most flaunting of the willows twists
as it grows. Its bark seems laid in swathes,
in foot-long feathers curling at their tips.
The only comparisons that come to mind for this
extravagance are those of men's artifacts –
the convention for fur in Saxon illuminations,
Leonardo's quilled and swirled descriptions of water,
the patterned joints of jousting armour, and
folk-tale memories of feathered cloaks the heroine
unwrapped from a walnut shell, the hero used
for his escape. I have seen nothing as wild
as this before, on the tree by the ford.

                          I assure myself
it's curious and beautiful but immaterial.
It only serves to hold my attention closer
whose attention is now obsessed with every tree
because they also do not move – the elms'
January roaring, the beeches like pewter marble
in their groves. I feel a sense of company
(not always comfortable, I assure you)
and of identity. And this tree more than others
draws me in – I stare at it, my back
to the ford where the children splash and call
in the sunlight, and find myself watching
flaked water, figures, riparian willows behind me
as if through fraternal and observant foliage.
Astonishment makes me turn. And then I feel
the carved and writhing tree observing calmly
my cold shoulders, my resistant spine.

Suburbia, Like Hanging

Suburbia, like hanging, concentrates
the mind most wonderfully, points here a view,
a slice of sky, a pattern of quiet roofs,
the observation of a sunset hue

that's moved across a wall as soon as seen,
the marks of rain's long action upon bricks.
Well, praise it for this excellent effect
it has on men – though these are city tricks.

Delight's always available to those
who need no burning-glass to urge the fire
of empathy; yet I still count my luck
for this suburban view of trees and spire

that faces afternoon and evening light,
is limited by lamp-posts, fences, lengthy wires,
but might be heart-of-Wiltshire scenery,
the smoke from chimneys autumn's last field-fires.

Pear Tree and Pattern

This was the way round it was.
I saw the pear tree first, in March,
one of an ancient row straddling
a hill. Pear tree twigs are short
and numerous, thick-budded before
bursting, pointilliste in appearance.
Then the new-ploughed field caught
my attention, each clod with its
attendant shadow, and the tussocks
taller by the hedge and also
stippling the ground between with
thicker presences. Whether I then made
comparison with an abiding interest
in early art or later on
I do not remember but it was near
that time, suddenly seeing in
sword hilts granulated with gold,
in clustered dots of ornament around
scarlet initials of manuscripts, round flat
wash representations of earth-bound
saints, thus elevating them,
the clotting of spring blossoms, the
dappling of the soil that infuses
delight and airiness into the world.

They had fresher eyes then and
more desperate winters, the men
who patterned thus. Spring brought
savour to a tasteless world; they must
have noticed this increasing texture
in the trees and on the ground.
Also, these patterns belong particularly
to the temperate countries
where spring's like that.

It Is Not Bred In Me

It is not bred in me to overlook
the close at hand, the particular.
I turn my head to gaze at every meadow,
to stare through every gate that's left ajar;

am always ravished by a width of view
but see the harebell at the bottom edge,
notice the thorn that gives the panorama scale,
brown roots, white garlic, beneath the tallest hedge.

It's just as well these are my inclinations,
to cry: Stop here – or here, that I may stare,
now that I have no choice but to travel slowly
or watch the seasons stroll from dark to fair.

For now I'm set in soul as well as tissue
and doubly urgent longing fills my days
to put down surely what is my obsession
– the small cold characters of plants, each phase

of sunlight on the grass, colour of thickets,
the shapes of leaves, the self-sufficiency of birds
– urgent because so relevant, their life's as strong
as ours and will outlast me and my words.

Ambivalence

This compassion contradicts itself, wishes to see
the abandoned cottage restored to dignity
of a dwelling, the atmosphere of use – a clothes line
stretched from outhouse roof to apple tree
on which the tea towels stir, the peg-bag weighs,
wood stacked by the kitchen door, mud paths
packed satiny by tread – yet would not lose
the overgrown corner by the spilling water-butt,
the thrusting meadow grass beneath the sagging fence,
or nettles that follow every human desertion,
raising tender standards of victory over the places
where men once dug or urinated or stored tools
and now do so no more.
        Also, to rip away the ivy
is to remove the last sweet autumn meal, the final
flowers of the season, to under-privilege late bees,
wood ants, bluebottles, destroy the shadowed
hibernation of small tortoiseshells and the promise
of berried harvest for the birds in bitter months.

South

Since sailing finished these must be
the loneliest seas in the world – Cape Horn,
Deception Island, the whole uninterrupted sweep
of latitude fifty south. Except for the odd
whaler or weather-ship, albatrosses only
frequent their surface; nothing hinders
the roll and collision of several oceans.
Unseen now, do they still exist? The men are dead
who sailed them but would have confirmed
their reality who held their ships
into the gale for weeks to round the Horn,
who burnt their hands on rope, who were
stunned by wet sails, who lay in misery in
swilling cabins to reach apricot continents.

Metamorphosis

The cottage people left the place
in early spring, shutting the windows tight,
taking the curtains down, all save
those above the sink, tissue-paper-thin
from years of steam – and also left
an apron, long-unused, hanging
like a ghost behind the kitchen door.
The woman took some plants, those
she had most loved, just showing green.
No sense, she said, to leave the roots
of phlox, forget-me-not, lad's love,
to be ground in by bulldozers.

But the demolition men were laggardly.
March became April, April May.
The sunlight strengthened, green thin shoots
began to palisade the path
with their frail shadowings.
Within the house, in musty rooms,
the warmth brought out some
hibernating flies and, from the folds
of that abandoned apron, one
small tortoiseshell who'd packed
her infant wings in that unlikely place
in colder months.
                    Later that afternoon
chance, or a stray draught in the shuttered house,
took her to the centre of the room
and light beyond the door
lured her to the equally airless parlour.
And there she stayed, fumbling
the small dull panes and resting
occasionally on the dusty shelf below,
already spotted with the excrement of flies
similarly immured, and harbouring
their concluding corpses. Cobweb
blurred the fine brown chequer of her wings
as she was trapped and struggled free
time and again from corners
of the spidered embrasure.

When, in June,
the first bulldozers breached
the walls, the long-staled atmosphere
exhaled, and breath
of scented summer was drawn in
too late. Dried abdomen
and folded drained-of-colour wings
lay tidily upon the window-sill.

Sapling Lime

Two years in the lawn and at last
it begins to look like a tree. Broom-head,
the children called it, lovingly mocking,
that first spring.

               Now I am learning its ways,
its family traits, its family likenesses.
Like all limes (but I had not thought
so young), it has a tendency to throw out leaves
haphazard up its trunk; also I realise,
watching this slim thing grow, why limes
give such abundant shade – its bright
and rough-edged leaves are set
in circular canopies that overlap
by lobe and margin, impenetrably lush.

Its winter form's as much a revelation
as its spring identity; its twigs
grow with a certain double curve
that's only then apparent, like fastidious fingers.
The line's familiar; I've seen it too
in thin fritillary leaves, in the flexed wings
of hawking martins and in the tapered paws
of cats cleaning the small circle of
their whiskered jowls. The link is strange
but obvious – perhaps if I were philosopher
enough I'd understand the natural ratio that
it illustrates in all these things but most
in limes, the tree I've chosen to outlive me.

Generations

No children see their parents in their prime
(the getting them was spice of that bright time);

so when another sixteen years have passed
and children turn enquiring eyes at last

upon familiar faces of their youth
they only see the middle-ageing truth.

They'll never know how long hair suited me,
how blond you were, how we walked amorously

down evening lanes in Somerset and Kent
(do they think hawthorn thickets were just meant

for present youth's philandering alone?)
Come now, they in their turn will moan

time's revolution, seeing their children's eyes
widen with that same disquieting surprise.

Button Oak To Arley

You would not think, on this quiet woodland track,
drama would be so near; but turn and take
the eastward lane that passes round the back
of that blue-painted cottage by the oak.
It keeps quite level for perhaps half a mile
then drops abruptly, its descent concealed
by its precipitation, alpine style,
between high hedge-bank, thorn, and barley field,

and comes on narrow meadows suddenly,
a wide fast stream, and wooded hills each side,
air thick with slanting birds, martin and swift,

– the River Severn shouldering steadily,
above the reach here of the highest tide,
secret and sensual in its oak-furred rift.

Wyre Forest

This upland's quiet, with little sound of men
and small variety of plant and bird.
Conifers are silencing the native woods,
ousting the oaks, and what is mostly heard
is what a Dorset man remarked – the sigh
of wind in supple twigs of evergreen
as soon as they are set.
                           The elements
inhabit this high land, this flat-washed scene
of forest, heather, distances; the airs
of every month here carry scents of spruce,
rain wipes the narrow leaves; sun encourages
the saplings' growth so fast it hardly spares
the last small fields. Now, any man would choose
a lowland farm, with sweet deciduous hedges.

Housman Country

These Shropshire marches carry his name
for those who know him well although
he was no native of these parts. Shropshire
for him was the sight and then the memory
of blue-ridged hills in the West, on the horizon,
seen from the field above his home
in Worcestershire; but his own particular
equivocal nostalgia lurks about these lanes
and blends most easily with what must always be
an element of difference for Englishmen who
travel the other side of Severn.

                     How his thinking
still pervades this countryside! Unexpectedly
one afternoon, exploring high land not quite
hills north-east of Ludlow, we came upon
a village football match. A grey sky pressed
from Wenlock Edge to Bredon, goal posts
stood white against the mulberry hedge,
the pitch was summertime's rough grazing, just
the size. Boys with intent and rosy faces
and jerseys bright as paint dodged in the mud;
the lane was packed with unexpected cars
and men leaned shouting upon gateposts,
roofs, and bonnets, loud and uninhibited.
We did not stop, for all the gaiety – we were
so patently outsiders – but had to slow to pass
and saw it all in one quick eager stare.

Now, what was there about that scene to
set the mind upon mortality, and unrequited love,
and distances of man from man? Only his images,
his words, echoing in the memory to make
a microcosm of a mucky country game.

Seminal Image

The Vale first took my sight of course
as we came over the hill like that
athwart the sunset thirty years ago.
A cobalt width and depth of distances
seemed to extend my sight in width and depth;
elms furred and striped the meadows lit
by the last slanting light and Cotswold lay beyond,
the lighter blue of higher land.

        I saw that first;
but, before we plunged into the valley's darker roads,
I glanced aside and was amazed
by hills on either hand, upon my level,
facing sunset full and brazenly, the miles of grass
like brass, like gold. Every hollow, track,
each tussock almost, thorns and junipers,
rabbit holes, chalkpits, old fortifications,
exposed themselves in detail, extending
bare and bright to evening light
and my astonished gaze.

        Such a sight
still moves me most, for various reasons
I do not define – landscape in last light,
viridian, bronze, and vulnerable, facing
and participating in the death of day.

Not the Dead of Winter

Not the dead of winter but the dying, late
November in fact and the trees quite bare
in the wood as we come, its condition
damp, its floor felted with leaves; and yet I swear
I smell violets, sweet in that biting air.

A foolish notion. All frost and snow are yet to come,
four months till spring and any expectation
of flowers among the trunks – and yet I smell
violets, so strong I look to see their station
beneath the hazels, their blue illumination.

London streets smelt like that when I was first
in love! Now it is nearly twenty years
and love's more sober. Not that, then. Just delight
perhaps so to be out-of-doors? Weekday fears
are soon dispelled as Saturday's reprieve appears.

I sit and sniff, knowing I'm mistaken,
but woodland smells are good, whatever season.
Soon we must go home, I know. I will not say
I have smelt violets without any reason.
We'll find them open in their proper season.

After the Apotheosis

The lovely music dies. The rose-pink
    satin's laid aside.
They are left alone in the gardens,
    the prince and his bride.

Beyond the walls where nettles
    breed butterflies
the talking fox that helped them
    silently lifts gold eyes;

the leather, inexhaustible,
    thonged bag is thrust
into a disused store-room
    to conceive, now, only dust;

the man who could drink rivers
    tosses back a beer,
hitches his trousers and ambles
    into Parchèdshire.

They did their duty, followed
    the story's track.
Now the magic's over. Earth, attic,
    meadow, take them back.

The Track to the Beach

The track to the beach was through
a wood – of thorn perhaps or tamarisk,
certainly tall enough to be dark.
The meadows this side were bright
and the sands beyond sunlit. Three years old,
I tagged along at the back and saw people
going down narrow paths, calling
to each other, laughing, in brilliant blue
and orange and striped pink
among the shadows. There were
butterflies seemingly tangled in the
thin branches; these were all blue.

When I read Dante first, many years later,
I saw quite clearly again the procession
of bright damned souls in the dark wood.

Upstairs Light

That particular light begins about half-way
upstairs – a brighter daylight than in kitchen,
hall, or living room, less overshadowed and reduced
by neighbours' walls or lilacs given their heads.
It sparkles. It floods the upper stair-well,
the austere landing, bleaches the bedspreads,
slides along walls, glares from the bathroom tiles.
I, at ground level now, remember it longingly.

Philosophically speaking, of course, it still exists
although, because I do not see it now, it seems
a thing of the past; I used to see, from upstairs windows,
the crystal bases of clouds, the sunset, the lupins
next-door-but-two, the winter stars. It lit
the morning ritual of making beds, of making up.
It spiced afternoon love-making. It illumined
the heads of children asleep.

It was a brighter world, upstairs.

Holidays, Explorations

How can I bear it that
journeying's over
while still the heart's un-
regenerate rover,

still longs to visit
strange hamlet, strange river,
to feel at view's width
the authentic shiver?

Now I must practise
good grace at parting,
to wish others joy though
I am not starting

the ride through the sunrise
to valleys of vision.
I fix on my smile now
with summer precision.

After the Requested Cremation

A steady north-north-west wind preferably,
though an east wind would do as second-best,
and so my bones' smoke and innocent ashes
would carry into Wessex or the west.

I'd like my dust to be deposited
in the dry ditches, among the fine grass of home,
on hills I've walked, in furrows I've watched making
in Wiltshire's chalk-bright loam.

If not that then Wolverhampton's chimneys
might send me Severnward; that would do instead.
Those rose-red farms, those orchards, have all been precious.
I'd like to fertilize them when I'm dead.

Make no mistake though, it'll not come to choosing.
There'll be a west wind in the week I go.
Or else my southern dust will fall on hated highways
and be for ever swirling to and fro.

Well, as I'll never know, it doesn't matter.
I'm not, in truth, romantic about death.
Only I'd like the right wind to be blowing
that takes the place of breath.

The Circle

Blackbirds are singing, the country over,
each in his own bud-clotted plot of land,
from central tree or roof or chimney-stack.
Each singing bird defies his singing neighbour:
this is my territory, these my lawns. Keep out.

It's a beautiful belligerence that rarely comes to blows.
Sometimes, clashing on the edge of territories,
they rise in twinkling combat (but without touch,
more ballet than battle) like black stars of the day,
and sink, and sing once more, and all
seems purely local.

                  Yet – come to think of it –
each bird hears probably three others, and they
three more. And so the circle spreads and
– to be metaphysical – one might say that
in the spirit, if not in the voice, each bird
hears every other blackbird in the land
and so the bird who shouts on the outskirts
of Stirling hears and is defying and replying to
the sweet carollings of blackbirds in Somerset.

The Double Nature of White

White orchards are the earliest, stunning
the spirit resigned to winter's black; white thorn
sprays first the bare wet branches of the hedge.
We should purely delight. Yet, when one
who gazes on this brilliance turns to look
into a companion's eyes, who gazes on the same,
he sees an evil look, as if of cataract.
This is but reflection of the whitely-gorgeous blossom,
but is uncomfortable, seems a malignity.

What's in white that's so ambiguous? for
the symbol of virginity is, too, unnatural
– like the albino animal, the parasitic plant,
and ghost. And bridal finery is gladly cast aside
for the colours of consummation.

Ah, after these white orchards, bright
and cold as youth and as swiftly shed,
will come through these same crooked lanes
(though differently positioned in the hedge
and on the verge) the green of tiny leaf, apples'
tender pink – carnation of bud and coral
of fuller flower – and then the creaminess
of pear, may, hemlock, crown of meadowsweet;
and we'll forget this leprous dawn.

Not until next year's spring will
the ambiguity of white so trouble us again
and then – again – only momentarily.

Migrants

I reckon that – give or take a few –
we send off almost a hundred martins
each year from this one house alone
to Africa in autumn. One cannot be
too dogmatic – but ten or twelve nests reoccupied
by the primal parents in April or May:
then the first brood laid, hatched, flown
– another forty: then the second brood.
These are in rather more danger, the days
shorter now, food not so prolific.
And some may die by cats, as well as suffocation
in the nest, or by starvation at the summer's end.
And sometimes eggs fall and break
before hatching. The yellow splodge on the courtyard
is not always explicable by overcrowding
in the muddy nest.

                    But we'll be optimistic.
Say, at the worst, that seventy go.
We've served our turn, done our duty
– never knocked down a nest, trying
all summer to keep the cats away.
More birds perish on the coming and going
but those that come back in the spring
reproduce, double, or treble the losses
(though they happen again, each year);
however, we help to keep the population stable
and the skies full, on blue June evenings
in the midlands, of sweeping triangular beauty,
of sweet, persistent, racial conversation.

Supplement

A few days ago, I heard the geese
go north. The sun still shone but
the wind was in the east. One could not
help but be sure that summer was over.

But then succeeded a few sunny days again
and the martins were bold and still
with us so that when they drifted high,
just feeding and calling in that unexpected blue,
free of all responsibilities,
their cries were like the sound
that smallest pieces of the finest broken china
shaken very softly in a basket of the greenest rush
might make, falling in tinkling drops of sound
about my head, above the house and the hill.

A few days more and then they, too,
will be gone. Blanketing silence about the house
will descend again for the next six months
as always.

But this was a good supplement to the summer.

Of May, Now

Of May, now, I can hardly bear to write,
so bright its untrod grass, so wide its light
I cannot share or only watch through glass.
This torture, though, will soon be done, May pass,
these bitter sweets be finished till next year
– the Botticelli days of green and blue, clear
to the horizon oak, the local blackbird's
final evening observation in sweet words.

Why, then, long for May each year? If it hurt
so much, why welcome it? Why not be curt
with sentiment, ignore rosebud and pink?
It is not possible. I only think:
Spring's come again, and I am glad! the trees
will shine again beneath May sun and breeze,
all bright with downy leaves, the gardens fill.

And will do, whether I am quick or still.

T.H.

He hardly ever looked directly at
the camera or the painters of his portraits,
though twice he nearly gave himself away.
Once, when old, in a Dorset lane, caught
off his guard perhaps, or proud
of the bicycle he held and forgetting
his reticence, he seems to be looking along
the hedge straight at the distant friend
with the camera; and once, again perhaps
betrayed by friendship, he looks up
– young, handsome, hair soft, waved back,
moustache most neatly trimmed – easily, as if
a friend had called: "Come on, Tom! give us a snap!"
(Though it may have been a studio set,
arm along the back of the chair, white gloves,
book neatly open on his knee.) In either case,
he remains elusive, gives nothing away,
body turned sideways, looking over his shoulder,
upwards certainly but sidelong, his glance
sliding past the lens and even going beyond
the shoulder of the photographer.

He looked down as he walked, too, friends said,
noting the patterns of frost on the road;
but we know from his work that he never missed
the beauty of a passing girl or the glint
of sunlight on distant farm-machinery.

His look is always the look of the proud
and reticent peasant, of the men who kept
themselves to themselves, whose masters
must not know too much about their men
– even though it be no more than a small superstition,
a family phrase, probably not even, at worst,
a bastardy. I doubt he had much to hide;
it was just in his nature to be secretive,
to remain lifelong the close boy from Bockhampton.
Certainly, before he died, he destroyed much
in bonfires on the lawns but probably

nothing as vital as we would like to think.
Men have always enjoyed bonfires.

Since I perceived this indirectness in him, though,
the younger portrait reminds me of a young
dog fox I met one morning slipping along
a hedgerow (he out late, I early). I remember
he glanced at me in just that way, independent
and unabashed, the handsome sidelong look
that went round and about but never directly
met my eyes, for that would betray his soul.
He was not being sly, only careful. That quick look
told him all he wanted – my kind, the direction
in which I travelled, even my intention. It was enough.
He was discreet; he had his own business
to be about, and a rich life several fields away.
He knew more of the land we walked than I ever would
– the slightest shadowing of slope in a field that
could camouflage a traveller, the brooks to be crossed
and used to break a scent. I presented no danger.

I see now how much alike these Wessex creatures,
fox and man, in their wariness were; for the latter also,
despite his downcast eyes, saw everything he needed
about his fellow-men and the world, marking it all
upon the full-mapped country of his mind and memory.

Envoi

Along the road to Ludlow
the limes stand bright and green,
in all the meadows round them
the lambs of spring are seen.

Spring calls me to that country,
to wander in its dust.
But chance takes others westward
while I lie here, and rust.

A Grey May

This is Shakespearian livery
– this sombre green and grey –
that his most wry-mouthed fool might wear
in some sweet-bitter play.
It suits *this* month of May

which only rarely has betrayed
the light behind the rain,
in evenings after tumbling days
of showers and storms in train,
when gardens shone again,

for moments only, before dusk,
and each leaf showed its soul
– a flattened sphere of lucent green –
about the lime's smooth bole,
or oaked and blue-belled knoll.

I like this melancholy though;
the fool's grey lights the gold.
Colour against such sober skies
looks warmer for the cold,
and dazzles above mould.

The Speckled Bush

In their natural state, their own Andean seed-bed, soil,
and atmosphere, these bushes perish in their time
in plumes of purple, go out in glory. And, in a cold autumn,
my own specimens do so too, although subject to
the restraining influence that English air imparts
to all its imports, so that the purple is a little less
extravagant.
                    This year, this spring, we trimmed
one of our seven flaunting bushes to keep clear my only view,
of spire and oak; the bush seemed bowed, I felt some guilt
at first. Strangely enough, we have been rewarded
in a most unexpected way (it will grow again next year,
in any case). No, what has happened is a change
of identity almost, for this autumn at least. The bush stands,
humbly and homely, at the corner of the house, no longer
wild as its brethren, but concentrated in a mass
of familiar colours, by an artistry close-worked
as in an English quilt.
                    And as I look at it,
with great affection, such a patchworked hump
(whose colours I can name in mostly English terms, not in
Peruvian purple) is what I see: dogwood, the brightest pink
we own, quarter-cousin to vermilion and to
crimson lake; and then a dulled Venetian red like
dried blood, a dye our Tudor forbears used in
wall hangings; and also blackberries not quite ripe!
These colours range so slightly they're not worth
cataloguing perhaps.
                    But now comes gold!
I feel I have variations to offer – here is cinnamon,
ginger, yellow pure as pyrites, topaz, amber like hair
or fallen chestnut fruit. And in between come all the greens,
some not yet started change, some finished it, so that
the bush is flecked with its basic colouring; but even
where autumn has moved in it is not wildly romantic
– at its best the desiccated blood I spoke of, at its worst
a dunnish yellow-brown not worth preservation.
But it has a sense of presence about it, although lopped.

I watched its quiet dipping one October sunlit afternoon;
an odd illusion seized me and has not let me go,
certainly not yet. I felt it was indeed a counterpane,
the colours so close because these were the only dyes
the Tudor fullers used; that it was lovingly herringbone stitched
to last – as it had; that it covered, in a back bedroom
subtly-sunlit, away from the noises of the yard,
a slowly-breathing, gently-dying ancient of the household
(his going easier perhaps because he'd always known this quilt,
even in days when some was still dress, cloak, curtaining).
I tried to dismiss the notion: who could be the withered man
dying without emphasis, like the bush itself, in layers of leaf?
Ah, I saw it again as a bush! Yes, that was right. But fingers
fumbled at a counterpane of country familiarities now
that I'd seen it thus. I was uneasy. I thought: when this cloak,
tawny as a fox, shall fall at last, who'll warm
the small cold spirit left behind, without colour or covering?

Ha! no frail spirit here, I think. Only old Lob would lie
easy beneath this naturalised and knuckle-headed bush
in the wuther of wind. No harm would come to him.
Mould'd warm him winter through, and then
spring bring a new coat, all gold, gold, gold!

The Syllables of Summer Birds

I lie as if five fathom drowned
beneath the bubbles of clear sound
my favourite birds let fall at dawn
about the house, above the lawn,
between the boughs of plum and pear,
further aerating that blue air.

These double calls, as sweet as rain,
circle our roof time and again –
the shadows of the floating birds
are all I see, but hear their words.
These conversations each sunrise
daily reanimate my skies.

Leftovers

The poem's done. I sit back satisfied.
But certain other subjects have been stirred
to life by its production, related
though irrelevant, eager to be heard

on their own account. As I reach, sighing,
for my pen again, a homely image thrusts
into my mind from several years ago
– baking day, and round my hands soft crusts

of pastry trimmings from the finished pie
which must be shaped and roasted with the rest
for these the children loved, indeed preferred.

Such bastard odds-and-ends are often best.

Trees

The old deer park across the road (wide grass
and no more deer) was, in my early years, inhabited
by taller chestnuts than they grow these days,
by shadier oaks and elms, by brighter birches.
I reverenced the first particularly, seeing the candles
heave, watching the sun across the fingered leaves,
and walked among them carefully at six years old.
The park's arrangement seemed to me quite paradisal;
trees were my youth's suburban pantheon.

I was a traitor to trees between my twelfth
and twenty-sixth year. War moved me to a countryside
that barely nourished them – the high gold downs of Wiltshire
with every skyline clear. The planted beeches
in their clumps, the narrow windbreaks, hardly interfered
with the long range of adolescent eyes. Distances
became divinity. Trees, I said scornfully, are
tangling shade, are flies, are tethers to the mind and view,
arboreal landscapes are the devil's snares.

Now I am back with trees though I cannot walk
beneath them. They tower like gods again as they did
when I was a child – Worcestershire elms and chestnuts.
I see in them now admirable examples that were not
relevant to me then, peasant virtues – their local patience,
their endurance of the dark. Agreed, they have no choice
so the comparison's alien, but not as alien as it seems
– they cry out when they're killed, like men.
Brotherhood now, then, whether I like it or no.

R. *Falling out of Bed*

That's how fooling often ends, you see –
giggling and talking after you'd been sent
to bed, fooling about
and falling out.

Oh but you're not hurt. I'm
only cross because I feared a broken bone.
Now settle down and sleep.

When the house is quiet again I
suddenly realise what flashed into my mind
hearing that tumble upstairs, that
bony bundling on the floor – the moment
of birth, the extraordinary sensation
of the limbs being thrust from my body
bundling smoothly out like the knobbed
rolling of apples in a sack and I almost
identifying then, in that excited moment,
the pointed chin, the symmetry of ribs, frail
elbows, knees, all tumbling into unexpected life.

On High, Apparent Land

Windmills were windmills once; wind set the sails wheeling.
      On high, apparent land at the edges
of towns, where the soil was too barren for farming
but the stone that made such excellent footings
and cellars was quickly struck, they sprouted;
and the citizens were only too glad of their services
to mind the climb. Some even noticed the view!
None relished the thought of them as dwellings though,
especially on the days, and nights, when all the winds
of heaven held high holiday up there. Only the miller
and his family (who knew the vibrations of their working home
to a hair) could appreciate to the full, though,
all the differences of sound and movement in the walls
when a full gale blew up; and the miller's wife
(brave woman to contend with isolation, odd-shaped
rooms, the constant stir of fire and stairs and steps)
could often tell, forebodingly, before her men,
what was to come, by the faster shadowing of her rooms
from the gathering speed of the sails, and the flight
of her fowls' feathers past the window panes.

And when it came – oh, any variation – the squeal of a timber
that could not be accounted for, that did not fall immediately
into some dark proper place in memory – made them all wince,
and look away, into the fire, or at some piece of work in hand
with more attention – and no-one spoke when the miller rose,
took his lantern down, and went, in silence, from the room.
Only when he returned and they saw, by the up-flung light
of the lantern and in the glow of the fire, his face untroubled,
did the family relax, breathe easily, begin to speak again,
and someone pass a comment about some happening in town.
For the moment, all was well; they'd pass the night
in watches, but, for now, all was well.

Stopping Places

The long car journeys to the sea
must have their breaks, not always
in towns where there's no room
to park but at the pavement's edge,
in villages, or by the woods, or in lay-bys
vibrating to the passage of fast cars.
The seat's pushed forward, the boot's lifted,
the greaseproof paper
rustles encouragingly. The children
climb to the ground and posture about,
talk, clamber on gates, eat noisily.
They're herded back, the journey
continues.
      What do you think
they'll remember most of that holiday?
the beach? the stately home?
the hot kerb of the promenade?
No. It will often be those nameless places
where they stopped, perhaps for no more
than minutes. The rank grass
and the dingy robin by the overflowing
bin for waste, the gravel ridged by
numerous wheels and the briared wood
that no one else had bothered
to explore, the long inviting field
down which there wasn't time
to go – these will stick in their memories
when beauty spots evaporate.
Was it worth the expense?
                but
these are the rewards of travelling.
There must be an end in sight
for the transient stopping places
to be necessary, to be memorable.

Gale in May

All evening I watched the restless garden,
the half-grown trees tormented to
the limits of their strength, the blossom
blown, no comfort, no serenity, no
point of rest for eye or spirit. Unquiet
as green ghosts bent on foretelling
destruction, they bowed and recovered,
seemed to catch a breath and bent again.

All night I dreamed of tall figures
falling in flashes of light,
across dark lanes, athwart terraces,
turning the heart with pity – people or trees?

Of 1959

Pink dress, pink shoes, pearl earrings,
dark hair pleated and pinned, walking
under limes, accompanied by
a dark and dreamy child, a fair
and vivid one – so, as I was ten years ago,
I would be remembered. But will not.

We play less part than we would like
to think in our children's memories. Of
that day, if anything at all, they'll remember
only the scent of flowers, myself
a tall uncoloured presence. The loving woman
in the chair, of later years, is how
I'll stay, and their father stooped.
Unless, as they grow old themselves, faint
glimmerings return, of a dark young woman,
of a fair laughing man.

The Condom in the Cart-rut

Not a ghost but what might have been
writhed at the dripping edges of the wood
when that spunk gushed; it lost its chance,
when this was dropped, ever to taste of blood.

Thin as the black rain and the dusk
it lingers there, dark eyes that might have smiled,
voice a man might have recognised,
the face that would identify a child.

But this stood fast, kept seed from seed,
saved girl from panic and a man from doom,
gave momentary ease to two
but to a non-existence the wood's wet room.

Lane and Poet

This lane's unique in England – no beauty spot, but just
a hundred yards of muddied verge, wide hawthorn-hedged,
    concluding
in a farm, a pear tree colonised by sparrows,
a tall grey house, unoccupied, dead-calm.
And this is really all, save for a dying plum
that's host to flowering ivy, swarmed with bees.
It is quite unremarkable, grey-green
and silent, backed by November trees.

But there's no other lane that's just this length,
has trees, house, grass in just this disposition,
or just these sounds – those sparrows, unseen ducks.
Such singularities give any landscape strength;
but these are references for my own odd vision
and my observing them its weekly crux.

Star Cluster

Suddenly – into the grey and February garden –
long-tailed tits! Rose, pale charcoal, ebony. Immaculate.
Detail precise as pen-work; curve of wing like a painted flat.
No especial seductions are set out to lure this sight
of small fierce beauty – only the normal and humane provision
for all who come, this cruel time of year.

                              The whole small flock
– six birds – descends upon one morsel in the apple tree, its speed
so sharp I gasp with surprised delight, so swift and sudden
the susurrus of the unexpected wings. Heads and breasts cluster
as close as the core of a star, in soft intensity, flinging forth rays
as from a star – those too white to look into for long,
but these fine black, though also quivering with power.
This movement is not heat, but hunger's urgency. The effect's
     the same.
The pattern that both make – a radiating circle – is that which men
have always used to symbolise divinity, or constellations,
or light and life; its short-hand still holds good. For though this
     group
of bright identities now darts apart, fast as flung stones, the parallel
remains, in air; they resemble coloured splinters, the fractured
     light
that's source of spectrum and rainbow, the paradox of the invisible
     fire
in the sunlight.

                         Now they re-unite, in the spiky excitement
of their small existences; and here's one identity again. The pattern
     is repeated
– that which signifies all brilliances, and can still be seen, in snow-
     flake haloes
of painted saints, in the margin of manuscripts, on icon and crucifix,
and the plastered walls of wayside chapels. It's also seen on
ancient sacred stone, in circles, on celestial maps – and in
my naked, green-mossed apple tree, against a winter sky.

Ashdown House

Seeing it first in time of war
I thought it that which gave it
oddity – no depth
against a snowy sky, black huts
on ragged lawns. It looked
ungainly, as many beauties
then were shorn of their power.

Now I have seen it again.
It still stands, quite irrelevant, in
downs which easily resist its
atmosphere, an awkward jewel
quite foreign to its setting
for all its lawns are smooth, its
trees in balanced vistas.

Elizabeth of Bohemia's cavalier
built it, after long exile,
seeing behind the chalk the tall
Dutch houses of the Hague,
homesick for exiled days perhaps
more satisfactory than those
last years when she was old.

A Latter Majesty

My garden's chiefest crop is moss –
this plot of land being the sweet green sink
for gardens half-a-mile away, up-hill.
It smothers, like a second skin, or pile on velvet,
all that offers any foothold for its grip.
Strangely, its most accommodating host, the finest wearer
of this panoply, is the garden's oldest inhabitant
– the ribbed, carbuncled apple tree, in its crowded
corner between shed and trellis, and bushes
that flourish as he has never done. His blossom,
and his fruit, have never been other than spare,
so perhaps he deserves this accolade –
particularly as it's at its best, and most surprising,
in the months and at the moment (just
– often, too, on days that have dawned dun
and so remained, until this final hour when, breathtakingly,
the sun breaks through the cloud) when no other prouder plants
        persist,
before actual dusk.

A long, low shaft of light slants athwart and through
his pushing neighbours – but it is he who's caught
in the spotlight, and stands forth, a figure in
skin-tight viridian, like a supernatural jester in a guise
so close as to be almost improper!

                            Who is this then?
this transformed and momentary monarch of our dusk?
Oberon? Herne? The Green Man himself?
He's gone as soon as seen – the celestial bodies,
whose swift proximity opened this corridor of light,
part company as swiftly as they closed; and sunset's done.

All that remains is a brown and rough-barked tree
(most un-divine, that had been Dionysos)
a sour, old piece of wood by the shed,
on which the uncomradely cats of the neighbourhood
                    clean their claws.

"Along the lane..."

Along the lane go two of almost
    equal height, her arm
through his. She takes my place, so sweet
    a surrogate no harm

enters my mind. Yet I can hardly bear
    to watch my daughter
on her father's arm. Salt in the wound.
    Fate gives no quarter.

"What is now..."

What is now my broken world
   is theirs new found,
the grass I eye so wistfully
   their paradisal ground,
and all things that die to me
   to them are immortality.

"The puppet cannot dance..."

The puppet cannot dance.
  All the nervous strings
are twisted, tangled, drawn.
  Through them pain sings

on one shrill ceaseless note.
  They cannot be put right.
Disabled now, the creature
  waits woodenly for night.

Mystery

It will be a puzzle to anyone who cares to sit
this summer beneath the chestnuts in the park
to find so many foreign twigs about their boles,
the shrivelled buds, the smooth, the ridgy bark.

But who looks up will see the black rooks' nests
and then recall perhaps those birds' peculiar tricks
of making homes from any tree but that which houses
them, collecting, miles apart, requisite sticks.

Eclectic as a pedant, one soars above the fields
to land, balance, and tug at other trees – knobbed oak, thin
sycamore – picking and choosing, dropping loot, bending
an awful eye on whoever dares to grin;

then, making for home through long blue washes of air,
brings one stout twig to add to the accumulating list.
It seems such wasted effort not to use what is to hand
but it's successful, there's no doubt. Black wings persist.

Oaks

A better poet than I
called them stiff-necked, and so they are.
Stiff-necked's the perfect epithet.
They boil in a high wind
because of this quality, the short twigs,
the sharply-angled branches, rearing
and returning suddenly, not
compliant with the gale in any way.

They grow immense in kindly
circumstances, with knobbed knees
and elbows patterned with moss;
but their stunted brotherhood
on acid soil's almost as impressive,
yielding to prevailing westerlies
only in so far as to grow slantwise
to the sea or the upland's edge.

This obstinacy's no failing.
They yield good wood after the several
hundred years that mark their prime;
they hold the soil and shelter
dynasties of birds. Their crooked
silhouettes on winter skylines
are signs of an endurance
beyond our capabilities.

Dead Fledgling

Honoured and exasperated by
the deft mud cones beneath the eaves,
we watched all early summer
the house-proud martins, thieves
of our early morning rest, sweep
the surrounding air the clock round
to feed the insistent mouths, the
darkening feathers, the incessant round.

Today the eldest fell. We'd watched
him lean far out, his head down-cocked,
a week or more, almost replying
to the children's quips, who mocked
kindly his hungry shouts. Just now,
from the window, I saw the black
and white, the soft plus-fours,
limp on the stones, with a broken back.

Bury him quickly now, before
the children get home from school, tell them
he's flown, they all appear alike,
the stub fork tails circling the hem
of evening light. Only he, so nearly ready,
will never know the desired feel of flight,
his life his wings, movement his condition,
nor get his living even in delight.

Paolo and Francesca

I cannot feel the fiery whirlwind's
such a punishment. Earth's love is lost,
agreed, but they are still together.
Such company's worth the being tossed

in hurricanes of hell. Their lips strain
each to each, their arms each other hold.
Is not that worth more than sitting quiet
in heaven's halls, alone, unkissed, and cold?

Frontier

All my life is lived on
the qui vive, expecting further invasion
from an insidious enemy.
I seem to be guarding
indefinable marches,
serpentine valleys like those
beyond Malvern, from frontier posts
on the hills, exposed positions
with for sentinel only
small courage and slightly
taller pride.

      Such slinking ways
he has! Waking one morning
I find he has infiltrated
another outpost or even withdrawn
an inch or two to strike again.
His armaments are quite conventional
– pain creeps up like a slow storm
between the mountains, uselessness
insinuates like small rain. They
do the trick though, are as hard
to counter as any heavier
weapons he might try: and my reinforcements
are puny and often unwilling
to back me up – really only
sporadic refusals to go down crying.

Proverb

I am determined not to miss
one nuance of the light
on spire and tree
this bright September evening.
So I sit and stare,
the washing-up undone, the cat
unfed, watching the sunset penetrate
pinnacle and bell-tower louvre
of the church, fine-fingered leaves
and conker cases of the golden tree.

The oak's oil-brown, the ash
still green. The grass I cannot see
must strike up damp but rosy-crowned
with the last sunlight
slanting down the hill. I cannot
go out into that evening but my spies,
memory and imagination,
report back faithfully. I recall
the Chinese proverb about selling
half of one's last loaf to buy
flowers for the soul but I wonder,
if I had the choice now, whether
I'd have longer years of ordinary life
or this half-life and the tingle
of senses extra-sharp to beauty
as now sit contemplating dusk.

"I have run, played, climbed . . ."

I have run, played, climbed,
    made love, given birth,
cooked, washed, devised a home,
    planted seeds in earth.

What more could a woman want
    than such life without tears?
Only to see it continue
    more years, more years.

Drug

I was served it
medicinally, not for kicks.
The effect was the same if
what I've read is true.
Such pristine colours, such purity,
in curtains I had seen for years
and knew had not been washed
a winter long: such easiness
of time, an hour, a second, all
reversed, all wrong, so that it
did not matter or was so long
boredom was active pain.
Things were very far away
– sheets, cups of tea, a yellow apple –
of such ease and importance
as they must have seemed to
Holy Roman Emperors whose servants
brought them immediately their faint desires.

It did not help the pain –
though that seemed bearable
and even beautiful at times –
but that particular significance of
each and every action, bird song,
music, trees against the sky, has gone
and now the old universe remains,
the misery as before.

I grew used to it again,
nor wanted its return –
that false beauty that had furnished
that false world, it was no
revelation of reality. I preferred
the old meaningless sufficiency, I saw.

The Brown Tree

"There's your brown tree!" Sir George would say,
gesturing complacently to some wide canvas
that neatly proved his point (most scenes did that
in his long gallery); and that worthy patron
of the arts, unassuming in looks but with
a triumphant gesture, brave though inelegant
that matched his theory (also widely known
to those young men – aspiring cognoscenti –
who visited him in hope of recognition,
now or yet to come), warmed to the praise of all
those aspirants who followed at his heels.
He saw his generosity of time would pay
in future landscapes from these murmuring admirers
and that his own pet theory of a central point
in any painted landscape would be taken up
and proved again and yet again. He did not let
himself ever pause to question its validity.
He'd seen it (as he wanted to) in many
early painted scenes, at home or in famous
foreign galleries. That central point that drew the eye,
the emphasis that would make sense of any shrubbery,
wide park, or woodland edge – why, there it was!
dark, distinct, preferably a tree, preferably
umbered – though black, or even a leafless oak would do
as well. Why, even Nature knew the part
that her offspring must play! If she did not,
if it were green, or gold, or even slightly off-centre,
that could be remedied; paint and imagination,
hand in glove, were quite excusable if satisfactory
to soul or senses. Artists before had neutered
Nature's inadvertence, untidiness, set
oaks where pines persisted, spoiling the moral
– that strength meant might meant right: and that point
could be made as well by umbered oak as by
wild scenes of Ancient Rome. Nature was triumphing
in this enlightened age: who questioned it?

Certainly none of those young men.

Airs, Air, and other Intangibles

These, then, are the highlights of my now-shuttered life
– the low and unexpected unseen sunsets, below clouds,
of days that had seemed twilight all the time
from clock-dawn till clock-dusk, grey and damp,
with quilted vapours overhead, and thick grass
dusk's darkening past green, and rose-tags in the eve
that will soon be night, and so the death
of momentary inspiration till
all such circumstances come again, again together,
day, dark, a final coral, upflung light.

These are the intangible sources now of much poetry –
light, colour, wind, the wet and low-burning copper of beech
    leaves,
mulberry hedge and ghostly spire, fogged branches
against a final coral cord of cloud.

The Elusive Spirit

He haunted my garden all the spring; but because
spring was forward (temperature and winds), the leaves
were also quickly full enough to check my seeking eyes
that followed the sound of the little, unfamiliar song
and could not fasten on any seen small bird as its source.
He kept me guessing, in my room in the garden, and often
I could not even turn as quickly as his song flitted away
through branch, bark, shadow, newly-unfurled leaves.

Well, he *must* have a name, I thought. His species I thought
I could be certain of – one of the warblers from that sweet
apparently-uncertain (but not truly so!) waywardness
of song; and his locale was insectivorous. So. A warbler.
But not one I knew; and I was afraid he might be off,
away again, before I could identify that little, patterned, sound.
Nothing fortuitous about it, surely it could be placed?
But none of the stutterings that attempted to reproduce
song, in the back pages of any ornithological books, quite fitted
this; and, oh, I was afraid he would be gone! (as the tits,
the long-tailed tits, are so soon come and gone from my garden,
only "passing through" – south/north – in spring and autumn –
such swift little beauties of corn-colour, rose, black, immaculate
          grey,
– no attractions to hold them just here, our slopes un-conifered)

He did not go. His song still sounded as the leaves closed thicker
on the bushes. His name? his name? oh, his identity? as if
it mattered all that much, save to this house-bound bird lover!
He may have visited each spring and I unnoticing before – but
this time he intrigued me – was he migratory, or had he
this year (as the winter was not really bad) overwintered here,
as warblers sometimes do?
               And still he baffled me until
one afternoon I saw him plain, and quite by chance, silent
at that particular moment but vocal a second before
and a second after. I was not even looking for him just then.
But there, clear between two layer leaves, a small neat body,
a black, velvet-as-moleskin head; and then he sang again,
and song, silence, sight, and song again fitted to the outline

of the skeletal words I'd read and named him Black-cap.
All credit to his unintended cheat, his innocent duplicity.
I hope his cunning keeps him sweetly safe
for many a day to come; he was a worthy opponent
and I am doubly glad that he outwitted me.
All the advantages were on my side.
I only won by an unworthy trick of luck.

Lime

Like a king whose garments are all set
with topaz cabochons, this tree's bark is all knobbed
and lumped with age, with cabochons also – but of
sulphur-coloured bark. He stands a moment,
inclining statelily to his ovation, like a ballet star.
The light moves on. Remaining where he is,
he seems yet to be withdrawing to the shadows
of the wings, emptying the stage of royalty.

Cloud

There are certain days here in October, when
the wind on earth's almost too strong for the inhabitants
– trees and flowers are knocked from side to side (the pace
at which each twig travels and returns depending on
the length and the number of leaves it still retains),
men and women are hurried willy-nilly,
from bus stop to shop, from van to house, from offices
to queues for further buses, clutching to themselves
anything unattached – hats, baskets, umbrellas.
Squalls accompany the winds; be prepared.
What is loosed, is lost, sometimes brought up unexpectedly
on tag or snag of branches, sometimes whirled into
normally quiet waters (that now achieve waves!)
and are doused and drowned and dead.
                              Earth
may be infuriating or fun – it depends
on one's age!
                    The sky's the loveliest place
to look, for any who have sheltered in quietude or
cannot choose but sit and watch; for what these
winds bring up – best towards the end of the day –
are clouds that belong to no other month.
The great white separate thunderheads
of autumn afternoons begin to link towards dusk and rise
from a long shared base of grey and cobalt
mist, distance on distance, with edges
the shapes of petals of anemones – curled and reflexed,
backed on each other in a constant silver shift.
                    The sun has left the earth
when the best of all is seen – from the last and longest
a peak stands up that's taller than the rest,
and looms. Perhaps it appears
benevolent to those quiet men who trudge down lanes
to home; certainly it's more familiar; but to others
who look up out of chairs, or catch a glimpse from as-yet
uncurtained landing windows, this form's malign
– as if it ponders breaking like a wave of Judgment Day,
smothering, foaming, and finishing earth.
It holds its shape, although seeds of light
boil within its outline, and lifts its crown

107

to the sun's final invisible refulgence.
Then that glow itself, at last, seeps
from the sky and brightness has gone.
The light that remains is grey, still, flat
on earth as well as above, except for that
white-filled (and ominous with internal silent
seething) shape above, its outline as clear as
an enormous flower against the greyer shapes beyond.
There is nothing else in the world of nature
that reminds one so much of a creature
of man's brain (though there was legend of some sort
behind that oceanic giant) – this apparition
– height, light, menace – resembles nothing so much
as the monstrous and pallid, wrinkled forehead
of Moby Dick himself, as he rose hugely
from the boiling seas to take a last revenge upon
the tangled boats and terror-stricken men,
catching cordage and all about him in his final rearing,
thrashing, humping a huge white shoulder
as he turns down again to those great depths from which he rose.

"The seed the hornbeam casts"

The seed the hornbeam casts
   will not be seen by me
to elevate from sapling
   into a graceful tree.

But though I leave the scene,
   as leave the scene I must,
I too have cast my seedlings
   into the human dust.

A Waking Dream

It looks like me, dead, in the road.
I seem to keep going back to make sure.
Yes, it's my old life, certain enough, like a
sloughed snake skin, patterned, significant,
still warm. I squat and stare into
the smiling face, enigmatic as a Botticelli
though hardly as beautiful. In the wet
hedgerow murmurs the first grey bird.

Dawn and pearled dust carpet the road.
My self lies soft. Soon full light will come
and then, perhaps, like Lamia, this
will writhe and disappear. Leave it now,
walk on. But of course I deceive myself.
That is impossible. It is I who will stay
while that grey shape will rise
and go and leave me in the dust.

Hastings

No chuckle-headed churls, these henchmen,
fighting one battle, defeating one foe,
turning in tracks to trek back the length
of that unhighwayed England, embaying
their strength at Senlac, to suffer,
defend, and die with their dear-loved king.
Free men these were, from muddy farms, facing
horses and warriors happy to hear of loot,
the whole unharried land before their hands.

A day they held them, dawn to dusk,
in marshy land; Malfosse pulled down mailed men,
arrows hissed slantwise from the sky.
And then the hooves harried the halt,
the wounded who went agonised away.

Drummed on the hooves, defiling, destroying,
but not what was worth, whatever
would serve them was saved. So riding
the victors revenged themselves on defiance,
the land was laid low and its law,
and its quiet kings of heroic qualities,
and golden marvels of its monkish manuscripts
– and Saxon was the century's blasphemy.

An Unrepeated Experiment

I never was so happy as that day
neighbours persuaded my mother I was in need
of Sunday morning church. I went reluctantly,
hated the hour or so in that tall space
(the inexplicable bobbing up and down, the cold,
the too-slow hymns, the nasal voice), was
only impressed by the much-rubbed nap
of once-embroidered hassocks, and so longed
to be outside that boredom was a pain.

Then we came out into May sunlight
and the cuckoo calling – and lingered on
the gravelled path to talk to regulars.
I hopped impatiently to see the chestnuts blow,
their candles rising easily on tossing boughs
as full-rigged ships in trade wind seas.
At last we passed the lych-gate, flinty wall,
cut across spinneys newly green, and came upon
knee-high buttercups, reflecting back the sun
from petals enamelled with his fire, spring-butter
blooms, dusting my bare brown legs with gold.
I stood to worship in that moving air.

I never was so happy as that day, at
six years old, to find that buttercups still blew
and burned outside uncoloured churches.

Pain Teaches Nothing

Pain teaches nothing except
the pure beauty of relief from pain,
eyes looking easily about once more,
the breath drawn slow again.

Nothing but pain matters while
it is present; music, sunlight,
the fate of children, are of no
consequence. Only the coming night

is extra agony, the body only fears
dark, silence, centuries of hours;
and even morning brings no interest
in food, warmth, flowers.

Pain teaches nothing except
the pure beauty of relief from pain,
– quiet sleep at last, and, on waking,
the spirit articulate again.

Molly Holden: A Memoir
by Alan Holden

MOLLY WINIFRED GILBERT was born on 7 September 1927 at 15, Linden Grove, Peckham, in south-east London, the first child of Connor Henry Gilbert, whose profession on the birth certificate is given as Commercial Traveller (Gas Appliances), and Winifred Sara Gilbert (née Farrant).

Her paternal grandfather Henry Gilbert (1868-1937) was a novelist and short-story writer at the turn of the century, some of whose general interests Molly was astonished to discover herself developing in adolescence – in archaeology and prehistory and in Celtic mythology, for instance. She later wrote a short article on him and his first novel (*Hearts in Revolt*, 1901) in *A Review of English Literature* (VI,4; October 1965). He never achieved popular success as a novelist, though reviews were generally respectful, but later used his learning (he was a typical late Victorian autodidact, able to read Latin, French, German, Anglo-Saxon, Icelandic, Welsh, Russian, Gaelic, and Italian) to retell for children stories of Arthur and Robin Hood, with the use of many original details drawn from archaeological and ballad sources, as well as Prescott's accounts of the conquests of Peru and Mexico. The Arthur and Robin Hood books were illustrated by Walter Crane. One or two of these volumes were in print, in small, cheap editions, a few years ago, and may indeed still be available; but as Henry Gilbert sold the copyrights to the publishers during a time of financial crisis – a fairly frequent occurrence – no advantage accrued to the family. At his death, a large library, including first editions of Gissing, an author whom he admired and who influenced his writing, was sold to Blackwells. A few books were kept and came to Molly, including a complete edition of Hardy's poetry (which she began reading when she was about ten), and old guide-books to early Britain.

When Molly was a few months old, the family moved to a new house in Wallington, Surrey. They lived opposite the old deer park of Beddington Hall, and some of her earliest memories were of the sunny sweeps of grass, the great horse-chestnut trees, and the wild corners. Her brother Anthony was born in 1930.

In her recording for the British Council in March, 1973, when she discussed her poetry with Peter Orr, and read a selection, she said that she remembered writing poetry from about the age of ten; no trace of it survived, but she was conscious of natural presences from an early age, and presumably this early poetry, like so much of her later work, dealt with this natural world.

In Spring 1940 Mr Gilbert lost his job in London and was offered a post, still in the Gas industry, in Swindon, at a much reduced salary. The family removed to Old Town, Swindon, on the hill, with its small shops and market-town air, somewhat aloof from the later railway development in the valley. The downs and sky, the ancient trackways, hill-forts and tumuli, the great prehistoric monuments – especially Avebury – were a revelation, and became a passion, to Molly. From this time dates her interest in archaeology and prehistory, and, as she wrote later, "although my descriptive poems now are mostly written about the Midlands, on the edge of the Marches, which are my present home, the spaces of Wilt-shire still lie behind all my poetry." Her explorations of the area were conducted on foot or by bicycle; this was wartime, and the roads were free from traffic, except for the occasional army lorry.

She was happy at the Commonweal Grammar School, being academically gifted, especially in English and History, though Maths was to remain a sore trial to her. She was encouraged especially by an English teacher; her reading was wide and unusual, including even the Ossian poems. And writing – in both prose and verse – was becoming important to her. A letter from the *Boy's Own Paper* dated 14 April 1942 rejects a story entitled "Day after Day" but commends the quality of the writing; Molly noted that it was a story of the Merchant Navy, written when she was fourteen and obsessed by the sea and ships. There were poems in the school magazine, and in the September/October 1945 issue of *The Poetry Review* came her first published poem, "Silence". In October 1945 Molly started an Honours course in English at King's College, London, where her love of literature increased even as she fed another of her passions: the history, personalities, and places of London. There are notebooks cram-med with her observations and comments. *The Poetry Review* pub-lished other poems at this time; one, "The Drowned Hebridean Fisherman", printed in the January/February issue, 1947, was read on the BBC *Time for Verse* in the spring of that year. One or two short poems were printed in newspapers – and paid for. Poems and prose appeared in *The Swindon Review* in 1946 and 1947, and in *Wiltshire Life* in 1946.

I first met Molly at King's in November 1947. I had returned from over three years in the army to start on the second year of my English Honours course in October 1947 – I had managed to get in two terms from October 1943 until my call-up at eighteen in May 1944, and those two terms were allowed to stand as one year towards my degree, since I didn't wish to start again at the beginning. I had to work hard to make up the deficit; a three-year stint in the army had not prepared me for the rigours of Anglo-Saxon. Molly was not a tremendous worker; she said that she couldn't concentrate after nine o'clock in the evening, though that did not mar her enjoyment of our numerous visits to the theatre, cinema, and concert-hall. From February 1948 onwards I went several times to her home in Swindon and was introduced to the Wiltshire countryside. Her enthusiasm for antiquity infected me. This was before the age when motoring was common, so that on a visit to Avebury we had the place virtually to ourselves, and drank in The Red Lion when it was still a thatched local pub, or stood on the eye of the Uffington White Horse to make our wishes for the future.

Molly was expected to get a First in her degree, taken in 1948. That she took an Upper Second must be due in some measure to the amount of time we spent together during her final year, even though I often pleaded with her to stay in and work – not that what I said had much effect. We wished to get married but decided to put it off until I had completed my degree in 1949. During this time, Molly lived with her parents in Swindon and did some paid work for the Victoria County History of Wiltshire, researching the files of *The Swindon Advertiser* for material on the growth of the town in the nineteenth century. Presumably this work is incorporated in one of the volumes of the V.C.H. – we never checked.

During the year, Molly suggested that after our marriage we should return to King's College for research degrees. I was doubtful at first, even though my interest in medieval language and literature was growing. Fortunately, however, Molly persuaded me and it became a matter of my getting a good enough degree, our obtaining grants – Molly from Wiltshire County Council, myself, as ex-service, from government sources – and fixing upon subjects for research. These conditions were met and in October 1949 we returned to King's to embark upon M.A. degrees. In those days it was a two-year course, requiring a substantial thesis plus two examination papers. Molly's subject was *The growth of interest in the antiquities and early history of Wessex as reflected in English Literature from 1500 to 1700*; I was editing some fifteenth-century manuscripts.

We were married at Swindon Register Office – neither of us was a churchgoer – on 17 October, and after a few days' honeymoon in Lewes (all we could afford as students), returned to our

119

research work in London. We lived for about six weeks in one room in Earl's Court, then found two upstairs rooms in the first garden suburb, Bedford Park, Turnham Green, in a house in one of the leafy avenues built in the 1880s by Norman Shaw. And here we stayed until we had completed our M.A.s in June 1951. Molly in a note refers to "those glorious early years of marriage". We spent most of our working time in the Reading Room of the British Museum, a privilege we both appreciated. I made brief forays to the Bodleian Library, Cambridge University Library, and one or two cathedral libraries, but most of the time we were together in London, working, visiting theatres and cinemas or listening to music, and sometimes taking afternoon breaks to visit Hampton Court, Kew, Richmond, or Hampstead Heath; glorious years indeed. Molly was writing very little at this time, though there was a short story published in *Argosy* in November 1950. She had shown me some of her poems just after we met, but no more for a long while.

After we completed our M.A.s, we left London and lived with Molly's parents in Swindon. I did various temporary jobs, and then in January 1952 took up a post teaching English at a boys' grammar school in Stockton-on-Tees. I lived in lodgings while looking for a place to live, and in the spring we moved into our first house, in Norton. We were again fortunate in the area we chose. Norton was originally a village, and, although now joined to Stockton by ribbon development, still had a green, a pond with ducks, a blacksmith's forge, and pleasant old houses surrounding the green and lining the High Street. Our small modern house, in a quiet cul-de-sac, faced an old brick wall boundary of one of the eighteenth-century houses, which had a garden containing enormous trees inhabited by rooks.

Our first child, Nicola, was born in February 1953, and Gerard in November 1955. With a house to run and young children to care for, Molly had little time for writing. In June 1954, she had some trouble with her legs and had to go to bed for about ten days. The ailment was described as peripheral neuritis. Whether that is an actual ailment or a euphemism I do not know, but looking back in later years we realised that this was the first onset of multiple sclerosis.

In September 1956 I took up a post teaching English at a co-educational grammar school in Bromsgrove, Worcestershire. There were not many houses for sale in the town then, though many estates have been built since. We were determined to live in the town, not in the nearby southern suburbs of Birmingham, so once again I lived in lodgings while Molly and the children stayed with her parents in Topsham, near Exeter; in 1954 her father had become area manager for Exeter in the South-Western Gas Board, thus severing, to Molly's great sorrow, the connection with Wiltshire. In May 1957 we finally moved into our house on the outskirts of Bromsgrove, where we lived until Molly's death, and where I still live. Bromsgrove is a small market town, blessedly not a part of the Birmingham conurbation; when we first moved in our house had old cottages and fields opposite and a farm further up the road. At appropriate times of day cows were driven past our front windows – a delight for small children. Though the area has become more built-up, it remains an attractive place in which to live.

We had little money, but children, home, books, the occasional visit to theatre or cinema, and rare holidays, made these years happy. Molly was beginning to write again; in December 1958 she won a *Sunday Times* poetry competition on the subject of Pasternak, who had recently been awarded the Nobel Prize for Literature, but had not travelled to Sweden to accept it because the Soviet authorities said he would be refused re-entry to Russia. Such love of one's native place found a ready sympathy in her. Several poems were broadcast on the BBC's *Midland Poets* programme in 1959, 1960, and 1961.

Molly's father died in March 1960. This was a great loss to her – indeed, to us both – and her feelings come out in a few poems. In the following year she began to experience difficulty in walking. In December I was informed by our family doctor that Molly had multiple sclerosis and would, in the not too distant future, become an invalid. Molly was not informed at this time of the diagnosis, and in fact did not realise until 1967, when she had been in a wheel-chair for over two years, the nature of her condition. Early in 1962 I began to learn to drive so as to give us easier access to the countryside. A legacy from a distant and unknown relative of mine enabled us to buy a car. Later it helped pay for alterations and additions to the house, when Molly could no longer get upstairs.

As Molly found it increasingly difficult to get out, so she turned more in on herself. Then began the flood of poems. Her first collection was a privately-printed pamphlet, *A Hill like a Horse*, published in 1963. As I remember, this was financed by one of Molly's aunts. It contained thirty poems, of which about twelve were reprinted in later volumes. Not many copies of *A Hill like a Horse* were printed; a few were offered for sale in a local book-shop, and of those only a handful were sold. The rest went to relatives and friends; I still have four or five copies myself. But paying to see oneself in print is an ambiguous pleasure, and Molly was not satisfied until her work had been accepted by a publisher willing to meet the cost. This happened in 1964, when Outposts Publications printed *The Bright Cloud*, a pamphlet of twenty-seven poems. The title-poem (first published in *A Hill like a Horse*) derives its name and subject-matter from Samuel Palmer, one of our early enthusiasms – indeed, years before, when we knew nothing of Palmer save a few illustrations in books, we made a reverent pilgrimage to the wrong Shoreham (Sussex, not Kent), and laughed at our ignorance later on. *The Bright Cloud*, too, was put on sale in a local bookshop and sold a few copies. Presumably it sold elsewhere, since Molly had one or two letters from people interested in her poems.

By now – 1964 – Molly was experiencing great difficulty in walking. In the summer, we had our last family holiday when she was still able – just – to get about. This was on a farm in Cumberland, near Hadrian's Wall. During our stay, we paid a visit to the Roman site at Housesteads, and the agony for Molly of walking the considerable distance from the car-park and having to turn back before reaching the remains is recounted in "House-steads".

At the end of 1964, she became confined to a wheel-chair (an electric one, procured for us by the good offices of our family doctor). She was just over 37 years of age, our children nearly 12 and 9. We needed much more domestic help, and this was before the days of attendance and invalidity allowances. Much worse than the financial difficulty was Molly's sense of misery and frustration. She was, in addition to being academic and creative, a practical woman for whom caring for home and family ranked high in the scale of values. Cooking, embroidery, garden-ing, pegging out the washing – all parts of her intense joy in life – now became difficult or impossible. She had never wished to take a job outside the home; now she had to watch as other women did for money the work in the house which she had done for love. That first year of disablement, 1965, was a bitter one, with little writing done.

Molly had never been a clubbable person. Now, although we had a collapsible wheel-chair into which she could be lifted from the car, she chose not to make many excursions. There was the occasional visit to my school, to a concert in which our daughter was taking part, a rare visit in the evening to the house of a friend, but in general she waited for weekends and school holidays, when we would go into the country and she could observe. There were a few faithful friends who regularly came to visit her, and did so till her death, but it was a revelation to both of us how many people whom we had regarded as friends never came, or came once and no more.

Her powers of observation were always remarkably keen, and now they were further sharpened by her enforced stillness. Domestic rearrangements had entailed building an additional room to compensate for a dining-room now used as our downstairs bedroom. The extra room looks out over a small courtyard and our garden, with views of grass, flowers, trees, bushes, hedges, the church spire, and a wide expanse of sky. This became, year in, year out, her world, of birds, changing seasons and weathers, to form what she called "the solid food of a curious poetry". She had now almost literally to "see the world in a grain of sand". It must have been towards the end of 1965, or early the next year, that she began writing poetry again. Thereafter, until a few years before her death, when the spread of the sclerosis took away from her even the power of holding a pen, she was writing hard, with only the occasional fallow period.

So our life continued, with the slow and difficult adjustments that the disablement of one of the marriage partners brings. We still tried to have family holidays in hotels with ground-floor accommodation, one being in 1968, at Blakeney in Norfolk; the poem "Cley Eye, 1968", in *Air and Chill Earth*, refers to the irony of a long-awaited view of the sea frustrated by our inability to get the wheel-chair up a high bank of shingle which cut off that view. After that year, we went on no more holidays together, the mental and physical effort having proved too much for her. But it was 1968 when Molly's true career as a poet began. In February, Cecil Day Lewis accepted for Chatto and Windus poems which Molly sent to him. Proofs came in June, and *To Make me Grieve* was published on 21 November.

Nothing in her poetic career ever equalled for Molly the excitement of three particular days: when she received the letter of acceptance from Chatto and Windus, when she received six author's copies on publication day, and when she saw her first long review in *The Times Literary Supplement* for 9 January 1969.

Headed "Excellence in Adversity", it occupied a full page and, while not ignoring some weaknesses, was most enthusiastic and glowing; no poet could have asked for a better reception for a first book. This was followed in the next few weeks by reviews in most of the hoped-for places, the *Observer*, *The Times*, the *New Statesman*, the *Listener*, the *London Magazinne*, and so on. Most of these reviews were good, although inevitably shorter and less satisfying than the first.

Just before publication day, Paul Humphreys of the BBC came to Bromsgrove to record a conversation with Molly about her life and work, and this was broadcast in "Woman's Hour" on 20 December. On 31 July 1969 "Woman's Hour" transmitted another broadcast entitled "Every day from my wheel-chair", in which Molly tried to present the feelings and reactions of a young woman whose life had been drastically changed by disablement. Its honesty makes for painful reading, but it was later of value to social workers who had dealings with disabled people. The poet George Macbeth, in charge of poetry at the BBC, came to visit Molly that July, too, and was greatly impressed by our ginger-and-white half-Persian cat (referred to in several poems), which he pursued through the garden in a vain attempt to make friends. As a result of this visit, there was a broadcast on the Third Programme on 28 November in which Molly introduced and read some of her poems. She began in 1969 to have poems published in numerous magazines and journals, including over the years the *Times Literary Supplement*, *The Review*, the *New York Times*, *Poetry Nation*, the *New Statesman*, the *London Magazine*, *The Honest Ulsterman*, and the *Listener*, as well as various annuals (*New Poetry* for various years and P.E.N. anthologies) and supplements (*Critical Quarterly* and so on).

Molly had also been turning her attention to prose. Her first children's novel, *The Unfinished Feud*, about Iceland in the heroic age, was written in 1967 and was accepted by Brockhampton Press for publication in 1968. She was told early in 1969 that it would be published simultaneously in Britain and America, and in August 1970 it was. Her three other children's books were published by Chatto and Windus: *A Tenancy of Flint* (1971) is a tale of an abandoned house in the Wiltshire countryside; *White Rose and Wanderer* (1972) concerns a boy who goes to sea in the early nineteenth century; and *Reivers' Weather* (1973) is set in the Scottish Border country in the late middle ages. As she said of these books, each of them celebrated and exorcised an obsession.

They were generally well reviewed and financially quite success-ful. In 1973 *White Rose and Wanderer* was adapted and read for children on radio. Two children's novels were written but not accepted for publication. *The Sun's Especial Summer*, written in the summer of 1965, is a tale of the supernatural involving a miz-maze, and *The Honey Length* – written in 1976 – is set in the late eighteenth century and the world of canals. The titles of these children's novels have always struck me as poetic and felicitous. Molly had it in mind to write another prose book – uncertainly adult/children's fiction – on the Great War, but never did so.

Early in 1970, Molly received an Arts Council award to help her to continue writing poetry. This she was certainly doing, and early the following year Chatto and Windus accepted her second book, *Air and Chill Earth*, which was published in November 1971. It was one of the Christmas recommendations of the Poetry Book Society. In her notes about her poetry in the Poetry Book Society bulletin, Molly wrote: "Sudden immobility in the presence of trees or certain landscapes was natural to me even in my restless days; now that this immobility is forced unnaturally on me I can make the most of it." She also referred to a note of bitterness in the poetry which could not be entirely eradicated. The reviews of this second volume, which I think her best, were again numerous and encouraging.

In 1972, Molly was one of the recipients of the Cholmondley Award for Poetry, and I went to London in May to accept it for her at the National Book League. 1973 was a busy and successful year: in March Peter Orr came to record Molly talking about her poems, and reading some, for the British Council. Two poems were chosen by Philip Larkin for the *New Oxford Book of Twentieth Century Verse*. She was invited to contribute to numerous journals, including the new *Poetry Nation*, based in Manchester. But 1974 was a darker year, overshadowed by serious illness; in February Molly had to be rushed into hospital suffering from a pulmonary embolism, and when she came out had a bedsore which, because of her immobility, took months to heal. This added to her already intense fear of hospitals.

Nevertheless, she was soon writing again, and in April 1975 Chatto and Windus published *The Country Over*, her final volume. This contained fewer, but longer, poems than the two previous books. For some reason – possibly difficulties with domestic help, which were harrowing in this and the following years – we kept fewer cuttings of reviews of *The Country Over*. Roy Fuller's in the

Observer was generous and perceptive. And that, except for some poems on the BBC TV late night "Closedown" programme, and some in journals, was the end of publication. As the sclerosis spread, life became harder still, until the final cruelty of her being unable to hold a pen and write. A cassette recorder was of no use; Molly was one of those writers, no doubt numerous still, for whom the flow from brain to hand to pen to paper was essential.

Our quiet pattern of life continued. Our children had left home for university, Nicola in 1971, Gerard in 1975. Holidays together were impossible; I took a five-day break alone in the summer, while agency nurses looked after Molly at home.

In 1981, however, I felt in need of a longer break. Molly agreed to go into a local hospital for about ten days. I went to spend a few days with our daughter in Tonbridge, now married and with a daughter Emily (whom Molly had seen when the family spent a few days with us at Easter). I was visiting some relatives near my home town of Gravesend on 5 August when Nicola rang to let me know that the Bromsgrove hospital had been in touch: Molly was very ill. I drove back to Bromsgrove, reaching the hospital at about 9.30 p.m. Molly died at 10 p.m. without regaining consciousness, immediately of broncho-pneumonia, though really of multiple sclerosis.

She was cremated, and I scattered her ashes on her beloved Liddington Hill, among the downs near Swindon.